Bringing Your Heart Home

The Harmonious Approach To Housing Yourself and Your Family

Vaughn Berkeley, MBA

Bringing Your Heart Home

Bringing Your Heart Home

First Edition

Vaughn Berkeley, MBA

Bringing Your Heart Home

Vaughn Berkeley, MBA

Copyrights & Digital License

The purpose of this book and this series is to educate. It is sold with the understanding that the publisher and author shall have neither liability nor responsibility for any injury caused or alleged to be caused directly or indirectly by the information contained within this book. Where every effort has been made to ensure accuracy, the book's contents should not be construed as a substitute for qualified advice. Statements regarding the content were taken from a variety of sources and may be subject to change.

Each person's needs are unique. Seek truth, seek a qualified professional to help guide you, but always follow your heart.

Publisher:
CM BERKELEY MEDIA GROUP
Ontario, Canada
First Edition

Digital ISBN: 978-1-927820-06-3
Print ISBN: 978-1-927820-05-6

Copyright

Copyright(c) 2015 Vaughn Berkeley. All rights reserved. Without limiting the rights under copyright reserved above, no part of this publication may be reproduced, stored in or introduced into a retrieval system, or transmitted, in any form, or by any means (electronic, mechanical, photocopying, recording, or otherwise) without the prior written permission of both the copyright owner and the above publisher of this book.

Any resemblance to characters, places, brands, media, and incidents are purely coincidental. The author acknowledges the trademarked status and trademark owners of various products referenced in this work, which have been used without permission. The publication/use of these trademarks is not authorized, associated with, or sponsored by the trademark owners.

Digital Edition License Notes

This digital book is licensed for your individual personal enjoyment only. This digital book may not be re-sold or given away to other people. If you would like to share this book with another person, please purchase an additional copy for each person you share it with. If you're reading this book and did not purchase it, or it was not purchased for your use only, then you should return to the online retailer or the author's website and purchase your own copy. Thank you for respecting the author's work.

Vaughn Berkeley, MBA

More from CM Berkeley Media Group

CM Berkeley Media Group, based in Canada, works with its authors to produce books which help to uplift the human spirit, spread the message of health and wellness, and offer practical insights in finances, and other areas. We also offer services to help authors convert their books to Kindle or ePUB format, get their book edited, and get a great cover design, and other services for independent authors.

Facebook Fan Page: cmberkeleymediagroup
Website: www.cmberkeleymediagroup.com
Email: info@cmberkeleymediagroup.com

Check out other great titles from our authors

For Adults

Eating4Eternity: Unlock Your Holistic Health Lifestyle.
Amazon Link >> http://amzn.to/1cO0kFd

Sweet Raw Desserts: Life Is Sweet Raw™
Amazon Link >> http://amzn.to/19msz2E

Can I Offer You A Cigarette: The Only Sure Way To Break The Smoking Habit
Amazon Link >> http://amzn.to/1enAfiJ

Colon By Design: Overcoming The Stigma Of Colon Sickness And Unlocking True Colon Health™
Amazon Link >> http://amzn.to/JGH05a

Fresh Food4Life™: The Case For Taking Back Control of Your Food And Empowering Your Family And Community.
Amazon Link >> http://amzn.to/J9yrQF

Bringing Your Heart Home

For Teens and Young Adults

The Youth Leadership Empowerment System™
Try out the FREE mini-course for youth.
Amazon Link >> http://amzn.to/1hRtMPy

For Children

The Adventures of Moshe Monkey and Elias Froggy: A Healthy Business (Book 1)
Amazon Link >> http://amzn.to/1QU7hxF

Moshe and Elias Build A Garden (The Adventures of Moshe Monkey and Elias Froggy) (Book 2)
Amazon Link >> http://amzn.to/1mI53Vn

Moshe and Elias Tropical Vacation (The Adventures of Moshe Monkey and Elias Froggy) (Book 3)
Amazon Link >> http://amzn.to/1mI4Amd

Living Foods for Boys and Girls (The Adventures of Moshe Monkey and Elias Froggy Book 4)
Amazon Link >> http://amzn.to/1QU6DQS

For more great info from the author, fun activities for your children, and more, visit: http://mosheandelias.com

* * * * *

Want to become a published author in 90 days? CM Berkeley Media Group has an online training program to help anyone aspiring to achieve this dream. Find out more about it and realize your dream at
http://cmberkeleymediagroup.com/writeyourbookin90days/

Dedication

This book is dedicated to those wonderful people who, like me, are yearning for a place to call home that is more than just a housing structure. This book to dedicated to all the people out there who want to get down in the mud and build with their own hands and create a dwelling place that was created with their own love, sweat, and energy.

To all the people living in cities in tiny apartments or worst condos, I dedicate this book to you. One day, may you discover your piece of earth that was set aside for you to build your dream.

This book is dedicated to all the good people who are longing to bring their heart home.

* * * * *

Acknowledgements

Writing a book is a very difficult thing to do. The book is a demanding mistress. She demands your free time whenever you are not otherwise occupied.

When you think you are finished, she demands more of the effort to tweak here, fix there, and to meditate and ponder. This book was written by the Fall of 2014. But this mistress demanded more tweaking, reworking of paragraphs, and slight changes to layout and design.

I would still be working on it, if I didn't say enough is enough. Thanks to all the people around to are my inspirations, my motivations, my supporters, and my reasons to laugh out loud.

Special thanks to:

Jean Booth, our editor

CM BERKELEY MEDIA GROUP, our publisher

Ian Lodge, a memorable Cal-Earth teacher

All my Cal-Earth family

My friends and family

And the ones I didn't mention here
but still have a place in my heart.

Thank you, all.

* * * * *

About This Book

This book is a book for dreamers. It is a book for those who have a dream in their heart to live in a better home structure. In creating this book, I want you to revisit the assumptions you have held all your life about conventional housing.

This book is not an instruction guide on building an earth home. However, it is a resource book that discusses the ways an earth home can save you money, save trees and forests, and ensure you leave a legacy for your children and grandchildren.

I do include very rudimentary project plan in the book to help you understand the broad strokes in your path to your own earth home.

Housing is your birthright. And an earth home could be your most expeditious route to claiming that birthright for yourself and your heirs and successors.

I've had people who know me calling me asking when I was going to build one at my place. They want to come and watch and see for themselves. Friends of friends have shown great interest in something so basic. It is a fascinating thing to behold. Let's love the earth again.

Inside the book you will find a few blank pages placed in odd areas. This is done on purpose. I did this for two reasons. First, I wanted to give you a space to pause and write your personal thoughts on what you've learned up to that point. Personalize the book with your own thoughts.

The second reason is that I always want to start a new chapter on an odd number page. So if the chapter ends on an odd number page, there will be a blank page on the next page followed by the beginning of the next chapter on the next odd numbered page.

So I managed to accomplish two things with one purposeful action. Rather than placing a lot of blank pages at the end of the book for our notes, you can make your notes periodically in the book.

Perhaps you will find the timing of the pause pages exactly where your heart and mind needed it to be.

My best wishes to you on this journey. Enjoy the book.

Vaughn

* * * * *

Vaughn Berkeley, MBA

Table of Contents

Dedication	9
Acknowledgements	10
About This Book	11
Introduction	15
A Look at Housing in History	21
The Trouble With Modern Housing	29
The Spirituality and Divinity of Homes	43
Social Justice and Our Tiny Homes Experiment	49
Returning to Our Earth Homes	59
Financial Impact of Earth Homes	67
Environmental Impact of Earth Homes	73
Build It and Your Life Will Come	81
A Sample Project Plan for Building	85
Loved It: Let Me Know	85
About The Author	95
Holistic Health Nurse Series™ Books	99
Great Resources	101

Bringing Your Heart Home

Introduction

Chapter 1

* * *

"Love begins at home, and it is not how much we do... but how much love we put in that action." - Mother Teresa

"As human, we have come a long way from living in open fields but we have lost the earth connection along the way. It's time to return to earth." - Vaughn Berkeley

* * *

People have lost faith in the housing model. According to a Los Angeles Times article in June of 2014, people were pessimistic about the housing situation and many still believed it was going to continue in a negative way or would get worse.[1] Given the current system of housing that exists in the general, conventional marketplace, I tend to agree with this outlook.

When we think about it, housing is truly one of our most fundamental and divine rights after being conceived and born unto this planet Earth.

From the moment of conception a beautiful place called the womb is created for the unborn child to reside. This home built of love, is nourishing, is warming, is protective, is communal, and is deeply spiritual. I believe if we were all to remember those precious moments spent within the tender warmth of the womb, we would find life outside the womb to be cold and unwelcoming.

The womb is a holy and sacred place. The womb is the first model home and spiritually and subconsciously it sets the standard for all of the homes that will follow for the rest of our natural lives.

Throughout my life I have been concerned about the quality of life of those around me.

Poverty and Accessibility To Education

While I was in university completing my undergraduate degree, I worked with the student government to create a perpetual bursary system that has raised well over $1 million for redistribution for students with financial need. And this bursary will continue to crate bursary funds for students every year for as long as the university exists.

My vision in creating that was making a university education affordable and accessible to those with a heavy financial need and a desire to prove themselves by accessing a university education. And the many students over the years who have accessed the funds may never even know of my vision for their success, yet their lives were touched by my actions over a decade ago.

For me, poverty is a very real concern that must be addressed through the use of a two-pronged approach. The first prong of this approach is educating the people. It is teaching them about the value of giving and about the value of sharing. It is helping them through educational involvement to make their lives better so that they may in turn make someone else's life better in the future.

The second component of this first prong is to create a systemic platform which continuously supports and reinforces the education of the improvement mandate of the first prong.

We accomplished this with a perpetual bursary system for the educational aspect of human existence.

However, education alone is not enough. A person must always have that sense of peace that is possible within the home. As human beings, I believe it is our goal and our deepest desire to re-create that security and peace that we felt when we first came into existence in this world.

And this is why my next objective in tackling the poverty dilemma is to teach people about restoration of the ideals of the sanctuary which is called THE HOME.

The Home

In the year 2014, we made a conscious decision in the magazine that I co-publish in Toronto, to run a series of articles based on the concept of tiny homes. When we developed this idea in the fall of 2013, initially it was just about teaching people to think outside of THE BOX HOME which has somehow become the standard of house building.

For four issues of the magazine, we would focus on a different type of tiny home to get people thinking about alternative options that are available to them when seeking a home.

But the journey became something beyond what we had envisioned back in 2013. In seeking to show others a different idea, we ourselves became changed as we discovered more about this topic and the series.

And in fact, I would say that I have found something that is beyond what I personally understood having a home to be. I discovered the spirituality and empowerment of the tiny home.

Big is not always better, as you will discover as you read through the various chapters of this book. You will also walk with me on a journey of enlightenment, of joy, of understanding, and hopefully of the fulfilment of the deepest innermost desires of your own heart.

Perhaps in the pages of this book you will find the answer to that question that has been gnawing away at you for as long as you can remember.

While I will present what I believe to be the only holistic option for spiritual and physical housing of your body, and while I had intended it to be a solution for the poor and displaced persons, and those in dire need of a place to call home, I found something that I believe every human being needs to reconnect with our true inner selves.

And this is why in my heart I was compelled to write this book. I could not stay silent knowing what I had discovered.

I could not let the opportunity slip by to tell readers, friends, family members, and anyone who would listen about something magical and divine in the way we choose to dwell and the place we choose to call home.

The Movement Is Happening

This is a global phenomenon that is happening. The earth will help to drive this building technology more mainstream in time. But I always fancied myself to be a person on the leading edge.

"Alabama makes strides in sustainable housing with first Superadobe dome structure in Morris" was the title of an article written about someone building their own earth dome.[2] The structure was modest but got lots of press exposure because of it's newness and unique approach to building. It's a reason to bring people together like they would in the old days for an old fashion barn-raising.

I believe in education and its power to effect change and so I hope this book brings to you an education which has slipped away from the human consciousness of the masses, but which is being brought back into the consciousness of individuals slowly but surely. I want you to have an "Aha!" Moment.

At the end of this book it is my hope and desire for you, that you will have a passion ignited inside your heart to discover the things that I have told you for yourself, and to create a safe place you call your home.
Enjoy the book!

Reference:
[1] http://www.latimes.com/business/realestate/la-fi-mo-survey-most-think-housing-markets-still-in-the-dumps-20140603-story.html
[2] http://blog.al.com/spotnews/2013/08/alabama_makes_strides_in_susta.html
.

Chapter Summary

In this chapter of the book we looked at the driving purpose for me to create and manifest this book into the world. I told you about my sincere belief that this could be one of the pathways to help lift a person out of homelessness and poverty. Ultimately, I hope to share with your that this book is an act of love for mankind.

* * * * *

Bringing Your Heart Home

Vaughn Berkeley, MBA

A Look at Housing in History

Chapter 2

* * *

"The ache for home lives in all of us, the safe place where we can go as we are and not be questioned." - Maya Angelou

"A home is our investment, not only in present lives but also in our future." - Vaughn Berkeley

* * *

Early Homes

Prior to the 1800s people would have lived in small homes that suited their needs. However, society began to change as we moved into the era of industrialization. The simple farm home with its modest design was no longer adequate for folks in the new approaching era.

But let's consider those early homes in Western culture.

Houses back then had a large kitchen and four small rooms. The kitchen area was an area to live and build the bonds that last a lifetime. Meals were prepared there and meals were eaten there. And perhaps some nice conversations took place before meals, during meals, and after meals. The wood fire stove also made the kitchen a warm room to congregate in during the colder months.

There was no need for a dining room or an entertainment room or workout room. The bedrooms in those homes were functional and compact. If you can allow yourself to imagine this type of home in a setting of today, people might call it a hunting cabin or their summer cabin.

Bedrooms were mostly unheated but the design of the

home lent itself to not getting too cold and the occupants often dressed warmly during the winter months, even to sleep. The furniture was hand made and was durable to last from generation to generation.

Sadly, today much of the furniture we purchase in the stores is created with planned obsolescence in mind. That is, it is designed with the intention of breaking or malfunctioning in a few years, thereby forcing the owner to spend money to replace the item.

People used candles or oil lamps in order to see at night. These lamps were not allowed to burn very long and so many people during that period got to bed early at night in order to have a good night of sleep.

There was no fridge; people had an icebox that had food on the bottom and ice on top, or if they could not afford an icebox, a bucket placed down a deep well could keep certain items cool for a few days.

There was very little wastage in the typical housing setting back then. People used their food wisely with little waste. What was left over could often be fed to farm animals for their food.

When a young couple got married they had to have the essential basics to start a new life together. These included a piece of land, a tiny house, a couple of horses, a wagon, a milk cow, a pig, and some hens to lay eggs and a rooster. Isn't that something? Back then, you had to start a family with the necessities to house, clothe, and feed the family.

This is very much unlike city life today which I'll discuss later. Many of these things would have been provided by members of the family to help the young couple start their life journey well. And as they got old and had their own children, they would also save some provisions for their children.

People were very closely bonded in that setting. Families lived close together and it was very common for the neighbours to have very good relationships with each other. If something went wrong on the farm, you could always walk over to your neighbour to ask for some help.

People stayed on the farm and worked on the farm because it was the means to sustain their life and their prosperity. There was no retirement age. You lived an active life until you didn't want to do it anymore. Some of the older folks would retire and live close to the city where there were many conveniences. They would rent out their farm in order to fund their retirement living in the city.

People were basically contented with their homes.

When we moved into industrialization and the post-industrial era, then human intuition about housing and life became warped and unnatural.

Consider that before, a young family needed a piece of land with their home in order to grow food and raise animals. Fast-forward to the industrial and post-industrial era, and people now are perfectly fine with living in houses that do not contain enough growing space to feed a family of 2 for a year. Also people replace what usable growing space they have with lawns that take up space, water, earth, and return zero food on that investment. Even worse, is living in an apartment with no land at all to grow anything.

The thinking has become so warped from the natural that people are paying enormous sums of money for apartments close to the subway instead of buying a home with some useful land. That young couple of the pre-industrial era knew that the land would feed them. A young couple in today's post-industrial era can only hope the supermarket has enough food whenever they need it.

It is almost like a psychological mind manipulation has taken place to cause people to desire that which appears to have value but in reality has little ability to sustain one's life and thus has no real value. And in this book, I'll point out where I think this happened to each of us.

With Industrialization and Post-Industrialization Came Unnatural Living

With the age of industrialization many people began moving off the farms in order to secure their fortunes in the cities. Those who lived and worked in the core often lived in small apartments with no space to grow food or to survive outside of the food supply system, the utility system, or the water system.

And this is true for the person today living in apartments in the city core. These people are 100% dependent upon the food supply system remaining intact in order to feed them. They are completely dependent on the utility company to provide them with gas for heat in the winter and with electricity to power their heaters and stoves. They are completely dependent on the water and sewage system to provide water and remove human waste.

And because of this dependency, like a user addicted to drugs, the mind of the individual will begin to form all sorts of excuses why they cannot make an enormous shift in their lifestyle. They will come up with excuse after excuse about why it is better to remain in their tiny prison of dependency.

Maybe you know of a person who will say that their little apartment (dwelling unit) is located close to work so they can't move. Maybe they say that the dwelling structure is located close to their children's school, so they can't move. They may say that they just moved in and don't have the money or the time to find another place to move into.

All of these excuses may have some validity in them, so I'm not calling them bull crap. The person simply is not ready to come out of their indentured servitude and their unhealthy lifestyle of dependency. Yes, the house where someone dwells plays such a big role in shaping their mindset.

I believe that a person's home is their castle or their sanctuary. If you live in a place that facilitates a slave mentality, then how can you possibly grow out of that mentality?

So while people were gathering in the major city centers, another interesting thing was taking place. Among the classes of workers, there began to be a trend in trying to define oneself as the more affluent person. So the sizes of houses began to grow to enable people to feel better about themselves and their unhappy existence.

Think about that for a moment. The house was meant to be an outward representation that you were doing something right and a validation that your life was not spent in vain for nothing.

Let's look at the data below of the median square footage of new single family homes between 1973 and 2009.

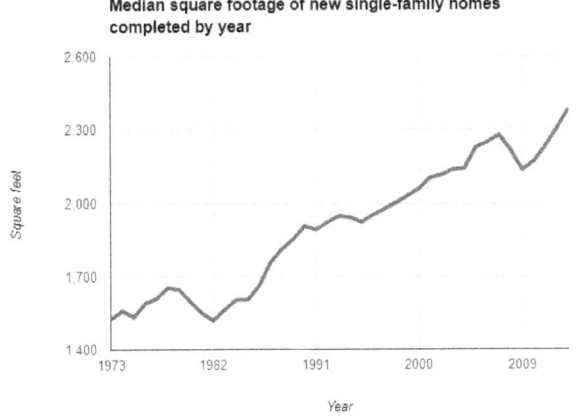

Source: US Census Bureau

You can see that the square footage of houses rose from

1973 to around 1980 then they began dropping until a low in 1982. From 1982 to around 2007, the square footage of houses continued to rise annually. That's 25 years of people being conditioned to want a bigger house in order to feel better about themselves.

Notice in 2008 and 2009, new home builders were building smaller houses and that this also happened in 1981 and 1982.

What do you think might have been the reason?

It may be due to a recession period that saw everyone tighten their spending. Thus, it was more economically feasible for the builders to make smaller houses for buyers during those recession periods.

The Path to Natural Living Again

Thankfully, we live in the information age now. We can put together the kind of lifestyle we need to be sustainable. There is a growing awareness about food security and the need to be sure you can grow your own food.

There is a fledgling movement underway to return to tiny homes. It is still on the fringes but every year more and more people are getting introduced to the idea. Our magazine, EternityWatch Magazine, covered various tiny house scenarios for the entire year of 2014. Every issue of the magazine in 2014 contains some vital information on tiny homes
.

Ultimately the pathway is yours alone to discover.

The culture that we have all become rooted in does not lend itself to true freedom, but rather a false sense of freedom that things like huge houses try to make up for. When we are disconnected from nature, we begin to feel a void that nothing can fill.

I see it as an opportunity for us to hit the reset button and try to begin thinking of living spaces that are 1000 square feet or less for a small family.

As more people catch on to this concept, we will have our natural resources because we will use less material to build. We will create less trash because we have less material being discarded as a result of building and furnishing a home, and we may well find the happiness we seek in a simpler way of living.

This book is about hope for the post-information-age folks. We can begin to heal ourselves and our planet again, and this healing starts in the home you choose to dwell in.

Chapter Summary

In this chapter of the book I have attempted to take you on a brief journey back in time to a simpler and dare I say better time. In doing this, I also gave you snapshots of our modern day living in order to compare and contrast then and now. I want you to see how the life has changed and also what has triggered that changed and help to socially engineer our thinking to what it is today. This chapter is also about hope and as you can see, we emphasize that the power and the choice is always yours.

* * * * *

Bringing Your Heart Home

Vaughn Berkeley, MBA

The Trouble With Modern Housing

Chapter 3

* * *

"When it comes to developing character strength, inner security and unique personal and interpersonal talents and skills in a child, no institution can or ever will compare with, or effectively substitute for, the home's potential for positive influence." - Stephen Covey

"The modern house is not truly a home. It is rife with things which fight against nature and mankind. Thankfully, people are waking up to the Earth again." - Vaughn Berkeley

* * *

We're Programmed from Youth

There are many things that I can see wrong with the way in which we perceive modern-day housing solutions. One of the biggest issues I have against modern-day housing is that it has been programmed by society into each and every one of us as the only way we can live.

For example, when a person is a young child, he's given numerous storybooks to read and he watches children's cartoons on the television or DVDs or computer today. In these pictures and images, each house is depicted as a building with a square base and a triangle top.

And his first images of these square base and triangle roof houses are reinforced again and again at every opportunity. Even when the storybooks do not consciously promote the typical Western society middle-class housing solution openly, they promote it subconsciously by making the stated housing solution seem impossible to obtain by the average person.

For example, the princess lives in a castle and some adventure takes place outside of the castle which causes the prince to show up and rescue her, and together they live happily ever after in the castle. When little boys and girls read that story, they know that they are not rich or famous as the character is in the story and therefore the castle as a housing solution will be one that is unattainable for them.

Parents continue to buy little dolls for little girls to play with. These little dolls often gather and congregate in a dollhouse. And what is the shape of this dollhouse? It is a square object with a triangle roof.

When children go to school and their teachers ask them to draw a picture of a home, can you guess what types of pictures they draw? They draw pictures of square houses with a triangle roof, and sometimes with a chimney on top that will be useful for the mythical red-suited man to enter the home during the holidays.

Sold on the "American Dream" or Middle-class Dream

Have you been sold on the dream too? If you're chasing the idea of living in your suburban house with 3 bedrooms, 2 baths, large kitchen and dining room, and a white picket fence, you've been sold the dream. Why do you need three bedrooms? Because you will need the space to house your 2.3 kids, of course. Even the Simpsons cartoon had the 2.3 kids television-program recipe.

Immigrants arrive on the shores of America or Canada in search of the North American dream sold in the form of the suburban house with a square base and triangle roof. And this house must be at least 6 feet away from the neighbour's house.

This is the same wherever people live in the world because the power of the movies and television to carry cultural and societal programming across borders makes it possible for adults who have never lived in Canada or America or England, to want to chase the "American dream".

This distorted vision of middle-class utopia is such a distasteful thing when one truly discovers that it is really like a little cell. A cell of your own in the block of cells, in the suburb, that you can call your own when it is not truly your own. You work so hard to be able to qualify to buy it, and when you do, then more of your troubles begin.

Deforestation

But before we get to the troubles for you, let's see some of the other troubles that the suburban housing sprawl creates. I've noticed this in Canada in the region where I live just outside of Toronto. The beautiful farmland that belonged to farmers for a long time is purchased by house builders. They get the land zoned for residential houses and they begin to build as many houses as they can possibly fit into that space. This involves bulldozing the land and clearing away the trees, shrubs, and destroying the natural habitat for the wild animals that live on the farmland in harmony with the farmer.

Trees are also cut down from some other places to make lumber which will be used to frame the house and construct it. When you consider it, the act of housing yourself in a house built using conventional methods begins with a lot of destruction of the land.

And if you opt to live in a condo within the city, you get the pleasure of living like a sardine in a can. The new game at that point is to pack as many people into as many vertical and horizontal cells (living spaces) as is humanly possible in order to squeeze every ounce of profit out of the structure.

Hazardous Chemicals (Formaldehyde)

Years ago we ran a story in the magazine, EternityWatch, about the chemicals used in the house and why your house may be a toxic environment. In laying down carpet, there are glues and adhesives that give off gas chemicals that are not safe for humans to be breathing in on a daily basis for weeks, months, and years. And as the resident of the house, living there, you and your children will be the ones breathing the polluted air for a long time.

Certain kitchen counters can sometimes contain formaldehyde. These too can off-gas, filling your home with the fumes on a daily basis, especially a newly constructed home. You, your spouse, your children, and your pets could all be breathing in this additional toxin in your air.

Then there are the paints used in the house. Unless your house builder is using very eco-friendly, low-VOC paints, they are probably using the cheapest paint (read high-VOCs) on the market to keep the building costs low. Which means you could be living with paint fumes off-gassing in your home for months. Even if your nose does not detect it, you could still be breathing it.

It Is Wasteful And You Are Paying For It

The huge elephant in the room that the construction industry doesn't share with you is that you are paying for a lot of wastage in new home buildings. You're basically burning through a lot of money as costs passed onto the consumer. Here's what I mean by that.

All construction sites have these huge dumpsters, correct? What are those dumpsters for? They are to collect the left over material from the construction of your new home. This is all stuff you paid for, by the way.

According to the research, an average residential construction wastes about 4 pounds of material for every square food of living space. That means a 2000 square foot home created about 4 tons of waste that goes into a landfill somewhere.

In simple terms, supposed you paid for 8 feet of wood for framing. But the builder only used 6 feet. The remaining 2 feet of wood gets thrown in the dumpster. Huh?!? But you paid for the 8 feet didn't you? Then when enough of those left over parts have to be taken to the dump, you pay for the transportation to the dump, the disposal fee the dump charges, and the rental fee to keep the dump on site.

But you never see those costs as they are built into the cost of your new home. They are hidden costs that you never take into consideration. And the wastage gets worst if you house has irregular sized rooms that needs more wood to be cut and more resources to be cut in order to make it work.

If your builder was a green builder looking for ways to save you money, they could probably reduce wastage by 20% to 50% but that is a more time intensive effort which most builders cannot afford or care nothing about.

If builders were not allowed to pass on that cost to the home buyer, I bet you they would become super efficient at saving those costs. But they don't so you the consumer end up contributing to more garbage in the world by have your new home built using conventional building materials and processes. And you pay for it too.

Relatively Short Shelf Life

Modern conventional homes built with wooden frames and hollow walls with insulation, and held together by tiny nails do not have a long shelf life. When you add in the fact that builders will attempt to shave their costs by using the cheapest materials possible, then you know you will have a house without a long shelf life.

A typical modern house can be expected to last about 30 to 40 years. That's about as long as your mortgage. And all throughout that time there will be things on your house that need to be fixed along the way. Repainting the insides of the house, repairing the tiles on the roof, fixing cracking siding parts, and repairing toilets and bathroom fixtures, are all examples of things that need to be done for the upkeep of the house.

My theory is that houses are built to be temporary. Many people don't feel the impact of houses that are built with planned obsolescence or *built*-in obsolescence because they will move from one house to another house within 7 to 10 years after moving into an initial house. Consumers are taught to purchase up as their financial situation increases and to downsize as they reach retirement.

This social programming forces people to keep moving and remain in the dark about the truth that modern conventional housing structures for the middle class are only meant to last as long as the 25- to 35-year mortgage.

After about 20 to 25 years and several owners, a house may be put on the market as a fixer-upper so that someone struggling to leave the lower class might have an opportunity to buy that home.

You can forget about passing your first home on to your children or grandchildren because if you have not sold it, it will probably be a wreck of a house. A home, NOT HOUSE, should be built to last 100 years in my opinion.

Prone to Natural Disasters

Modern conventional homes are built with the philosophy of taming the earth or fighting against the earth, and thus when the earth fights back, the house loses, and business and commerce wins. I'm sure you remember the devastation caused by Hurricane Katrina in New Orleans. It made all the news headlines about the incompetence of the first responders, the challenges of the many people left homeless, and so on. But the homes that were destroyed were demolished and rebuilt eventually.

Can you guess what type of house was built? A square box with a triangle roof. Is this like banging your head against a wall and hoping the wall will move each time? The definition of insanity is doing the same thing over and over and expecting to get a different result from the previous time.

If you look at any natural disaster zone, you'll hear people talk about rebuilding and making things better. The community comes together, people help each other out, and the builders come in to build. And they end up building the same square base and triangle roof, wood frame home. The home owner appears happy because their house is restored.

The builders are happy because they got paid on rebuilding. The banks and insurance companies are happy because they can make money on the deal. In the fog of happiness, no one asks the simple question, "Isn't that the same type of house that broke the first time?"

You can also expect that it will break again when the next natural disaster hits. The house owner expects this too, so they buy more insurance to protect the new house because the recent loss is still fresh in their minds.

Recently, a tornado caused damage to the town of Angus, in Ontario, Canada. The townsfolk now have the task of rebuilding. News reports were first about how scary the entire ordeal was, then they moved on to the great response of the emergency workers, then the great community of support, and now on to the time to clean up and rebuild. This is a great cycle for the mental and physical challenge ahead in the coming months.

But I can guess what kind of houses are going back up, can you? Yup, it's houses with square bases, triangle roofs, and held together by nails.

As if things could not possibly get any worse, the town of New Tecumseth, in Ontario, was also hit by a tornado within only a week following the Angus tornado. New Tecumseth is located close to Angus.

Now the cycle has to be undertaken.
1. Sadness at the Loss
2. Happiness for the Emergency Crews
3. Happiness for Community Spirit
4. Motivation to Rebuild

And then it's back to the same old houses that are prone to the same attacks of nature. I think by now humans should have gotten the point that nature can defeat those types of houses; but alas, that's the only thing most builders know how to build, and that's the only concept most people have of houses.

So the ignorant are doomed to repeat the mistakes of the past because they are unaware of any other options. But you are reading this book so you will learn of other options.

Financial Burden

A home is a heavy financial burden for many people who live in conventional houses. In fact, it is so burdensome that a large proportion of wage slaves (average working people or working poor) decide to rent because they cannot afford to buy a home.

STOP the fallacy of this thinking!

I had to throw that out there because I firmly believe that everyone can afford a home of their own. And I believe it is a divine right of every human being to have a place of their own and a home of their own. It is not a divine right to rent someone else's housing structure. You should be warned that if you follow the conventional thinking of a system that is designed to flow money from the poor to the rich, you will not have much money.

Vaughn Berkeley, MBA

Burden #1: The Mortgage

A mortgage, in 1913 was also known as a dead pledge. Mort meaning death and gage meaning pledge. It signified that whatever benefit of the property there was to the mortgager was lost or dead to him if he should breach the pledged agreement.

Today we call a mortgage a bank loan for a house. But if you were to think of it as a dead-pledge to the bank, how many people would rush to sign up for that? Not many, I think. So the concept has been sanitized in order to make it common and acceptable to the average person.

In order to qualify for the dead-pledge (mortgage), you need to be making a certain amount of money annually plus you need to have a sizeable down payment. This is already burdensome and an invasion of your privacy. And to make matters worse, the interest on the mortgage is many thousands of dollars. This is money that could have helped you increase the quality of your own life.

An example from a mortgage calculator available from a Canadian bank:

Mortgage size: $300,000 (this is the house value)
Mortgage term and type: 5-year variable interest rate mortgage (currently 3%)
Mortgage length: 30 years
Payment frequency: Monthly

Using these values, the calculator told me that in a 5-year term, I would have paid $42,000+ in interest charges, $33,000+ in actual loan repayments, and I would still owe the bank $266,000+ at the 5-year mark.

The numbers (rounded to thousands):
Interest Paid: $42,000
Principal Paid: $33,000
Balance Due: $266,000

Now a young person could tell you $300,000 - $75,000 = $225,000$. But you or I would still owe $266,000, not $225,000. And $42,000 is a lot of money you've lost by paying interest on the dead-pledge (mortgage). You could buy a car, travel the world, or put away money for your kids' education with that money.

And that's only for 5 years. You still have 25 more years on the dead-pledge (mortgage) to go. All the while, you or I will be bleeding money every month and every year until the dead-pledge (mortgage) is cancelled.

Using the same mortgage (dead-pledge) calculator, I put in making a bonus payment of $5,000 on the principal annually.

For the same 5-year term, the numbers (rounded to thousands) are as follows:
Interest Paid: $40,000
Principal Paid: $60,000
Balance Due: $239,000

You saved yourself $2,000 in interest payments and reduced your balance due by $27,000. But $40,000 is still a lot of interest; don't you agree? The bank calculator told me I saved $58,000 off my mortgage and reduced the payment time by 10 years. But notice I paid $100,000 cash to the bank and still owe $240,000. No wonder the middle class stay poor and working hard.

You can try these exercises yourself. Just go to your favourite search engine and type in mortgage calculator and play around with the numbers.

So this enormous financial burden that causes you to lose tens of thousands of dollars every 5-year term is one major drawback to buying a big home. This one makes your banker rich.

Vaughn Berkeley, MBA

Rent on Your Property

The government charges you rent on your house called property tax. Think about this for a moment. If you are 60, 70, or 80 years old and you no longer work, can you stop paying property tax on your home? No, of course not. If you don't pay it, the government will attempt to seize your home for non-payment of property taxes even though you are retired. This is wickedness. And it is an unjust system. I believe no one over fifty years should pay property taxes on their primary dwelling place.

Property taxes are one way you lose money. This tax is tied to the assessed value of your house. So if your house is worth more, you will be assessed more. What do you think drives up the value of your property? It's the darn mortgage (dead-pledge). Easy access to money inflates the value of the house which causes it to be taxed more.

Heating and Cooling Costs

Another drain on your finances are the ongoing costs associated with using your house.

The triangle roof houses are typically built with the long side of the roof facing the southern sunlight in Canada. This means that the house heats up a lot during the summer months. In fact, you can't stay in the upper part of a two-storey house during the summer. The heat becomes unbearable by around 2 pm. So how do you control this? You attempt to control this by installing a home cooling system that regulates the temperature. This sends up your electricity bill during the summer months.

If the house was simply built on a different angle, it would be a lot cooler during the summer and would not require high cooling costs. But this is bad for builder profits, bad for heating and cooling companies, bad for the electricity company, and bad for commerce. So you have to endure the heat in the summer and contribute to the commerce.

During the winter months, these houses can get incredibly cold and so must be heated. During the winter of 2013, we had some terrible snow and freezing rain. It caused trees to fall and knocked out the power for certain areas of Toronto and outlying areas. For about a week, my friend who lives in Scarborough, had no heat in his home. He and his wife had to go stay outside of the city with a friend who had heat. It was an unbearable time for many people in Toronto and the affected regions.

Suppose you lived in a house that has a gas fireplace and a furnace. You could heat your house with the furnace during the winter. It gets incredibly expensive with the extreme cold. And the gas fireplace is also expensive to keep going. The design of the house lends itself to this additional cost.

Water and Sewage Costs

You also lose money every time you open your tap. You pay a water service charge and a sewage charge. This adds up to many thousands of dollars over the course of your life in your house. You also have something called a lawn which you have to maintain. Your neighbours expect you to water it regularly and so you pay for the water to pour it on your grass which gives you no benefit whatsoever.

That is just wasting your money. It's much better to plant an edible garden and use your water to grow your food. At least you will get some return on your investment of your time and your money.

Household Maintenance

You'll have to replace things that get broken around the house. You'll have to repaint from time to time. A broken furnace or a broken toilet seat or faucet, or caulking in the

bathrooms are all examples of things that come up. This is another way you have to spend money.
Are you satisfied that you're bleeding money with a conventional house?

No Connection to Earth Bio-Electrical Grounding

Another aspect of the toxicity of modern houses is the isolation of humans from the earth. Ancient writings state, "from the dust you were formed and to the dust you shall return". Today, scientists are able to tell the earth has a bioelectrical field, it has a gravitational field, and other things. When builders ground a house, they attach a house to the earth. You can even see some roofs with a metal rod on them that has a wire running into the earth. This grounding removes unwanted electrical energy from the house and lets the earth take it.

The earth also has an impact on human beings. Scientists can now measure the impact of walking barefoot on a human being over the years. Being in the modern houses of today cuts off the inhabitants from the earth. There is always something between you and the earth. It could be wood, or beds with high wooden frames, it could be a synthetic mattress, it could be carpet covering wood floors, and it could even be house slippers.

Face it, the modern house which fights against nature and disconnects you from nature changes you on a sub-atomic level. It is on a vibrational and frequency level that science is only just understanding. Some of the recorded negative impacts include joint pains, inflammation, increased stress, low energy, hormonal issues, and so on.

This decreases your body's healing propensity while increasing its propensity to succumb to sickness. Thus again, it is causing you to make your doctor and your pharmacist richer with each visit and prescription.

Chapter Summary

In this chapter, I've highlighted many of the inconvenient truths about modern-day houses that are never told to people. They are an example of systems built upon systems working together against the human being for which they were supposed to benefit. And it is unjust and a reason I feel so strongly about speaking up about it. You need your eyes wide open for this enlightenment to occur. Now that I have shown you the dark side of modern housing, the rest of this book will show you the light side.

* * * * *

Vaughn Berkeley, MBA

The Spirituality and Divinity of Homes

Chapter 4

* * *

"The strength of a nation derives from the integrity of the home." - Confucius

"Peace of mind comes from a combination of being in harmony with heaven and earth, with living in a home that is your sanctuary." - Vaughn Berkeley

* * *

It's Spiritual

Believe it or not a person's house is a very spiritual place. A simple search on a popular Internet search engine for the term spirituality in homes brought up over 13 million hits. Many of those hits included things like retreat centres, articles people have written, websites advertising everything to do with spirituality and homes, and more.

It would appear that as the world continues to evolve and our collective consciousness awakens, we are seeking more spirituality and meaning in our lives and our everyday places. And there are many sayings which represent the way we traditionally have felt about our home. There is a saying that a man's home is his castle. And another saying suggests that the home is a sanctuary for those that dwell there. Even the ancient scriptural writings of Judaism dealt with many aspects of the home.

And according to the Bible and the Jewish scriptures, at some point God dwelt on earth among humans. It is recorded in the Scriptures that the house in which God dwelt

Bringing Your Heart Home

had to be designed according to his very specific instructions. His house would be called his home on earth.

The very first instance of this recorded dwelling place of the God of heaven and earth was the design given to Moses after the children of Israel were freed from the bondage in Egypt. And this house of God was deemed to be a sanctuary.

And as man is made in the image of God, according to the Scriptures, so too must the house of man be built and furnished as though it were his sanctuary. Whether you are a man or a woman, a small family, or a large family, it is of utmost importance that you would choose a place to dwell that supports you and your family in your spiritual journey through time and space on planet Earth.

For the purpose of illustrating the spirituality of the home in this chapter, I will use symbols of what I believe is a representative of the model home perfected. In these models we seek to realize spirituality as a key element of peace and prosperity, joy and safety, health and vitality, all returned to the home environment.

The first place I want to draw your attention to is the womb. Every human being should be able to form some sort of imagery in their mind about the womb. And indeed many women will be able to capture a deeper sense of what I am trying to describe in this example.

The womb is the ultimate sanctuary and home environment for a human being on planet Earth. Think of it for a moment. The womb is created and prepared without human hands. When it is ready for its human occupant to take up residence, it is a place that provides everything necessary for proper growth, health and wellness, warmth and comfort, nourishment and sustenance, and joy and companionship.

Yes indeed, all of these things are provided to the unborn child in the womb without any reservation. The womb as a home is the safest and most loving environment on Earth.

But most importantly the human being that resides inside that womb-home is joined to that home in a manner which sustains the life of the being.

And using this example to illustrate the point, we begin to see that the shadow of things we call homes today are nothing more than desolate places. In fact, I would never call a dwelling place that is made within a square base and triangle roof a home. I call it a house, or housing structure, or dwelling place because a home is much more than a physical structure. A home is a place where the spirituality of the human being becomes interconnected with the dwelling place and thus forms a home.

The second example that I will use to illustrate the point of a home with spirituality are the plans for the sanctuary that were given to Moses by God, Yahweh. I'll refer to it as Moses' Sanctuary. The Scripture says man was made in the likeness of God, therefore as God's home had significance on earth, we can draw some lessons for our own homes.

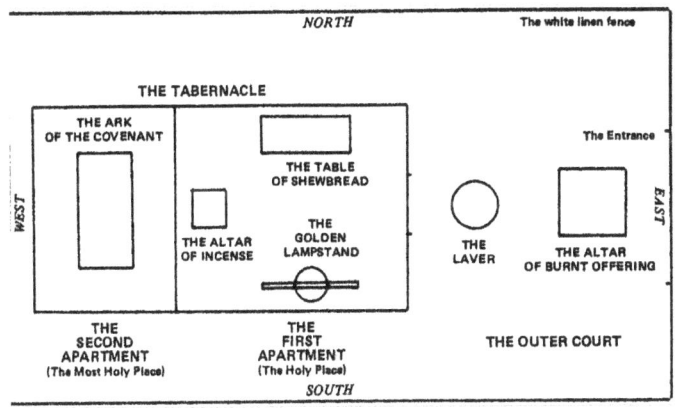

In Moses' Sanctuary there was a white linen wall that surrounded the entire enclosure. And this wall had a single opening or doorway. The doorway was on the East wall. It was the only way by which humans would go in or out of Moses' Sanctuary. As you walked through that doorway, you came to a place called the Altar of Sacrifice/Burnt Offerings where forgiveness for sins took place. This forgiveness of sins represented a cleansing of the soul or spirit.

Beyond that was the laver, a huge bowl with water for washing. Then there were two apartment areas joined together. These were the Holy place and the Most Holy place.

The Holy place was an area for spiritual food and sustenance. That represented a place where the prayers of the human would be taken up to God. The Most Holy place was the place where God dwelt. It was his resting place.

That sanctuary Moses built contained a lot of symbolic meaning for the people as a nation and for humanity, but there is also something for us as individual persons, and as families within our own homes.

Now if we take those two places that I would call a model home and combine them into one element that will serve as the basis for building our own home, we can extract parameters for building our own home for maximum spiritual impact in our daily lives.

Essential Elements for the Spiritual Home

1. A Place To Connect With Earth and God
2. A Place of Comfort and Safety
3. A Place That Is Not a Financial Burden
4. A Place That Is Durable
5. A Place To Recharge Your Body, Mind, and Soul

Note that the womb of a woman is prepared for its human inhabitant without human hands. We are unable to achieve this with our earth home so we will do the next best thing.

Our home that we construct will be prepared with human hands but will be inviting and full of loving energy from the labour of those involved in its construction.

Vaughn Berkeley, MBA

Note a Bit More About The Elements

<u>A Place To Connect With Earth and God:</u> In the womb, the mother becomes like a god to the preborn child. The mother's role is ever present. The mother is the sustainer of life to the preborn child. The mother is the protector of life of the preborn child. The sound of the mother's heartbeat provides a sense of rhythm like the ebb and flow of the tides. The umbilical cord connects the preborn to "earth" or to the mother and simultaneously with "god" the mother who sustains the preborn child's life. We mimic this in our earth home by ensuring there is a connection to the earth and grounding. We connect with God by integrating spiritual elements into the home as well.

<u>A Place of Comfort and Safety:</u> Modern houses can stand up for years but are just barely able to survive a natural disaster. With the construction of our earth homes, our goal is to build something that works with nature in order to endure and last two lifetimes or more. Thicker walls, designed to consider the elements of earth, water, heat(fire), and wind, we will have a place of comfort and safety.

<u>A Place That Is Not A Financial Burden:</u> Just as the womb is not a financial burden to its preborn human occupant, and the House of God built by Moses was not an ongoing financial burden, so too, our earth home must be constructed so as not to be a financial burden on us. There will be an initial upfront cost of building as with any housing structure but this cost will not result in a 25 or 30 year mortgage. A dead-pledge (mortgage) is a grievesome financial burden to place on a human just to have them own a home which is their divine birth right on this planet.

<u>A Place That Is Durable:</u> We touched on this before but it is worth repeating. In building our earth home, we design a home that will be able to last 150 or 200 years. These are homes that we can feel proud to pass on to our children and grandchildren and our great grandchildren. When they walk through the home and touch the walls, they must be able to

feel a connection with you. They should be able to feel that your hands touched the same wall that they are touching now. This gives a rich sense of heritage and belonging that too many of us are missing today.

<u>A Place To Recharge Your Body, Mind, and Soul:</u> As human beings we get tired from all our work during the day. When we get tired we need to rest. But who can rest these days will all the burdens of life. Our earth home must become something of a shield against the nonsense and daily grind. When we use the earth and live in a structure designed to function in harmony with the earth, we can feel more at ease inside of this home. When you walk on the floor or touch the walls, you can feel the grounding connection to the earth. This grounding sensation will help to recharge your body during the night so you are prepared to meet the challenge of the next day.

Ideally, you want your home to be like a womb to you. You must feel at ease in the structure. You should have no worries about a burdensome debt load, no worries about toxic chemicals, not a care when you are in your sanctuary. But in order to achieve this, you have to take the steps to plan and build this sanctuary.

Chapter Summary

In this chapter we covered the spiritual aspects of the home as we are spiritual beings living in this earthly realm. When you combine the spiritual elements of life into the place you desire to make into your home, you can reap the benefits on a level that is more than just physical. The whole becomes more than the sum of the parts.

* * * * *

Vaughn Berkeley, MBA

Social Justice and Our Tiny Homes Experiment

Chapter 5

* * *

"I believe that being successful means having a balance of success stories across the many areas of your life. You can't truly be considered successful in your business life if your home life is in shambles." - Zig Ziglar

"Home is the foundation where lives are built. When government leaders, public, or private enterprises do anything which destabilizes the home, it is like committing genocide." - Vaughn Berkeley

* * *

A Holistic Lifestyle Magazine

I'm co-publisher of a local Toronto magazine called EternityWatch Magazine. The magazine reaches about 20,000 readers each quarter and is available in print, digitally online, and in the iTunes Store for iPad. The magazine is focused on a truly holistic approach to life and especially health and wellness.

The magazine is the brainchild of my partner, Jenny Berkeley. She's a nurse, a health educator, a certified holistic nutritionist, a raw food chef, and has been on television and the radio. She's an award winning chef, a best selling author, and a local Toronto celebrity. Her passion to help Canadians understand that the path to health is taking responsibility and control of their health destiny, led her to create the magazine.

As co-publisher, I had my input on the Tiny Homes series.

Bringing Your Heart Home

In 2013, we decided that in 2014 we would run an experimental series. We'd focus on the Tiny Homes series as many Canadians would like to live in something that is affordable given the rising costs of housing and the dismal increases in salaries.

Our goal was simple. Give our readers a new idea for housing in 2014.

We wanted to help our readers think outside of the wooden box (pun intended). After all, the conventional houses most people live in are nothing more than wooden boxes held together with nails. Can you think of another wooden box that people are buried in?

The first article we selected to feature was on a gypsy type of house. It was a very tiny home built on wheels so that it could be hitched to the back of a pickup truck and moved anywhere.

We made contact with a Canadian builder of these types of gypsy caravan homes and she agreed to write an article for us on the topic. Jenny and I even visited her home where we saw a couple of the caravans in production. It was quite an experience and you can read the article written by the builder in the Winter 2014 issue of the magazine at http://eternitywatchmagazine.com/magazine-store/

The second article we decided to feature was again about a single-person type of dwelling. This one was a yurt. We contacted David, who purchased his yurt and lived on his parents' farm in Ontario. He wanted to preserve the natural layout of the land so the yurt was for him, the perfect option.

A yurt is made of fabric but the company that makes these uses space-aged fabrics so it is a far cry from the types made by primitive peoples. David's story was also a very interesting idea for our readers to consider. The yurt is moveable as you need to dismantle it and pack it to go to another area. It is not as mobile as a gypsy caravan. It is a bit more expensive than a gypsy caravan, but it has more square footage. This article ran in our Spring 2014 issue of the magazine: http://eternitywatchmagazine.com/magazine-store/

The third article was written by me and the experience I must say has altered my perspective on life and housing.

Firstly, I always believed that having a house of your own is a fundamental human right. No human being born on this planet should be homeless. But the major problem or hurdle for me was: How do we help people to connect their fundamental human right to a home with the empowerment in order to manifest that home? And how do we do it in such a way that everyone from the poor and working poor to the middle class can all have the same opportunity?

In 2012, I learned about the concept of earth homes, but the opportunity never arose to go to the institute to learn. That was, until our 2014 Tiny Homes Series.

It completely transformed my life when I saw the missing piece of the puzzle. With this type of housing, I understood that all human beings can now have access to housing in an affordable way.

And the writer in me just wanted to write about this and share the concept with the world. Hence, you have the benefit of reading this book.

Here's the interesting thing. Our readers got very excited about the concept. I got people requesting more magazines and stories came to me of people wanting to build these types of homes in Africa, Peru, and other places. It really got buzz going.

The article I wrote about the earth homes can be found in our Summer 2014 issue of the magazine at http://eternitywatchmagazine.com/magazine-store/

Bringing Your Heart Home

The final article in the Tiny Homes series was on cob homes. It was written by our regular magazine writer, Derryck. He's been a regular supporter of the work we're doing with the magazine. And when I asked him to research a piece for me on cob homes, he was only too happy as this was something he personally had an interest in. Derryck's article was very well put together as I didn't realize some of the old European cob homes have sold for over a million dollars and they were over 200 years old.

This type of home is out of reach for most people, but to build it yourself as a person looking to get into your home leaves room for possibilities. The cob house article was published in our Fall 2014 issue of the magazine: http://eternitywatchmagazine.com/magazine-store/

We wrote a final wrap-up piece putting it all together and connecting the dots for our readers in the 2014 Special Edition of the magazine published in December 2014. This issue was our very exclusive edition with double the page count of the regular issue. The issue can be found at the Apple iTunes store for iPad.

The Lessons Learned

For me and those of us on the EternityWatch team, the biggest lesson learned was that there is a big need among people to have a housing solution that is a true asset to them and not a financial burden.

When a person is young, they need a home of their own instead of paying all their earnings into rent. When a person is older, in their senior years, they need a home that is mortgage free and low maintenance. There is a real need for the knowledge of building a truly holistic home that is sustainable and beneficial.

I personally am enamoured by the concept of a home that can last for a hundred or two hundred years with only a minimal amount of effort. This is a home that can be a legacy to your children and grandchildren or even great-grandchildren. Wouldn't it be nice to be able to leave a home like that to your future descendants?

When your great-grandchildren stand in front of the house you built with your own hands, they can look at it and say, my granddad or my grandma built that.

When they touch the walls, they can almost feel your presence as you laid it. This, for me, is building a home now to touch the future where you cannot physically reach.

It's funny that something as simple as an idea for a theme to help meet a need in others could turn out to be such a life-changing experience for me too. And this is my hope for you in reading this book. I want you to have a fantastic dream and know that it is possible to make it become a reality.

Can I reach out and touch my great grandchildren? Not physically, but with my own earth home, I'll be able to communicate my love to my future progeny.

Can you dream of a big housing dream for yourself too? Dream it and manifest it.

Social Justice

A few years ago I was presented with an award that recognized my dedication to human rights and social justice at Ryerson University. To this day, I am still honoured to have been recognized for something that I sincerely care about.

The scripture notes that the poor we shall have with us always.

Then I say to you if anyone has chosen the path of eliminating the burden of poverty for human beings, then that person has chosen a good path.

Bringing Your Heart Home

It may be a path filled with hard work and few successes but every human being lifted out of poverty along the way is another blessing added to the individual, the community, and our beloved country.

Just recently I read an article that filled me with horror and sadness. The headline stated, "Homeless woman fined for building her own home" and this grabbed my attention immediately so I clicked on the story. The sub-headline stated, "Darlene Necan says she's been made to feel 'awful' for trying to house herself."

According to the story, Darlene was a member of the First Nations, more specifically the Ojibways of Saugeen First Nation. Darlene had become homeless and spent her time couch-surfing with family members and friends. Yet her spirit would not allow her to quit even as a 55-year-old woman living in dire poverty and living off the kindness of friends and relatives.

She finally decided to try to lift herself out of her terrible condition by returning to the piece of land where she grew up. On the very spot where her parents' home once stood, she decided to build a small one-room cabin as her home.

Unfortunately, somehow since her childhood to the present age the land had been reclassified as Crown land, that is belonging to the government of Canada, instead of part of her aboriginal heritage.

She called her little home her castle. It may have been small and very modest but it represented hope to escape the trap of poverty for this woman. She built it using materials that were donated to her from those who knew of her struggle.

Now this poor woman is at risk of having to pay up to $10,000 in fines if she loses her court case. This horrible situation reeks of the injustice that so many living in poverty face in their lives.

Vaughn Berkeley, MBA

Homelessness and Poverty Are Systemic

York University's Canadian Alliance to End Homelessness estimates that 235,000 Canadians per year go through a period of homelessness, at a cost to the economy of $7 billion.

And for many people, homelessness is not about being lazy, making bad choices, or being unlucky.

According to a new study by St. Michael's Hospital researcher Dr. Stephen Hwang, published Oct. 23 in the British medical journal The Lancet, Hwang argues that "homelessness is equally the result of structural factors within a society, such as systematic inequities in educational and employment opportunities, a shortage of affordable housing and social policies that are targeted against marginalized populations."

The Canadian Alliance to End Homelessness gives the follow ten points to eradicate homelessness:
- Planning
- Data, research and best practice
- Coordinated system of care
- Income
- Emergency prevention
- Systems prevention
- Housing focused outreach
- Rapid re-housing
- Housing support services
- Permanent housing

These 10 points are excellent points to address the systemic condition but they can also be used in conjunction with earth-home building to address the short-term housing need.

Using the system of earth homes and emergency shelters, we can address the factors of Emergency Prevention, Systems Prevention, Rapid Re-housing, and Permanent housing.

Bringing Your Heart Home

As long as people are not looking for a huge home based on conventional thinking, earth homes can be smaller homes, with fewer expenses and resources, can be built quickly and will be a massively effective tool in the fight against homelessness in Canada.

It is my belief that this can propel Canada (or any other country in the world that wants the glory of actually doing something) to be a world leader in addressing this issue.

Any head of state that implements this correctly will be remembered as a giant in history. Communities need to work together to bring this to the attention of leaders at the local and regional level.

Disaster Relief

Just as I was preparing to publish this book I received word via the magazine on the earthquakes in Nepal. As most people around the world knew, those earthquakes were severe and resulted in the loss of many lives and countless homes and building structures. People were literally left dead or homeless.

However, in that chaos and despair, I very pleased to receive word of the Pegasus Children's Project which built a children's orphanage in the northern Khathmandu valley of Nepal. A UK organization, Small Earth, built over 40 domes in 2006 for the Pegasus Children's Project in Nepal, which is home to over 90 children and their caretakers.

Small Earth's founder, Julian Faulkner, shared the news: "The domes have come through relatively unscathed with just surface cracking to the plasterwork… in the village below the site 15 houses have collapsed and many others are badly damaged with all the villagers now sleeping under tarpaulins in the fields."

This report came in after the first earthquake in Nepal. And it is a testament to the strength and resilience of the earth home architecture developed at Cal-Earth in California. The Pegasus Children's Project in the northern Khathmandu valley in Nepal survived the 7.6 magnitude earthquake on 25 April 2015, and the structures are all still standing.

As the earth experiences more of this kind of weather, consider the housing you currently live in. Is it too hot during the summer months forcing you to use your air conditioning? Is it too cold in the winter months, forcing you to use your heating? How resilient is it again tornadoes, and earthquakes?

The earth home technology has been published by NASA, endorsed by the United Nations, featured in countless world media outlets, and awarded the prestigious Aga Khan Award for Architecture in 2004.

The caretakers and the children were safe throughout the ordeal. The domes survived with only minor plaster damage which is easily repaired.

This story filled my own heart with gladness. To see that earth homes are able to withstand the earthquakes and that those precious orphans and their caretakers are safe and sound. This is what a home is supposed to be. It is a sanctuary for those who are discarded in society. It is a shelter in the time of storm. It is a refuge for those seeking safety and comfort.

How can you continue on in your daily grind of modern North American living and not question what's the point of all this rat-race living? There is a silent disaster in North America too! It's not an earthquake but it is impacting millions and millions of people who are living in a shattered and broken existence.

You need to wake up my friend. Wake up!

Bringing Your Heart Home
Chapter Summary

In this chapter, I've introduced you to our motivation for doing an entire year of tiny housing articles as part of our experiment. It is an experiment in awakening the consciousness of people to the new possibilities. We've also seen that systemic poverty and homeless is like warfare waged on segments of the population, namely marginalized groups. If we desire a just and equitable society then addressing the housing situation with earth homes must be a higher priority.

Links
[1] http://www.cbc.ca/m/news/canada/thunder-bay/homeless-woman-fined-for-building-her-own-home-1.2824688

* * * * *

Vaughn Berkeley, MBA

Returning to Our Earth Homes

Chapter 6

* * *

"A girl phoned me the other day and said... 'Come on over, there's nobody home.' I went over. Nobody was home." - Rodney Dangerfield

"We all want to connect and we try so many ways; social media, meetups, networking groups, and yet we remain disconnected to the biggest part of our lives. Connect to truth and other connections will be fruitful." - Vaughn Berkeley

* * *

Our modern-day society has so many advancements which on the surface seem to be such marvels to benefit mankind, yet some of these marvels have yet to achieve the long-term benefit to match the short-term benefits they give.

Earthing

Earthing is an ancient concept. It is based on the belief that we are connected to the earth from which our ancestors were spawned. And the earth itself has a rejuvenating energy which we can tap into if we allow ourselves to connect to the earth.

The Unlucky Horseshoe

Before I tell you about how we have been disconnected, let me talk about the horse. You know the expression, you've got lucky horseshoes. The horseshoe is used in some cultures to represent a symbol of good luck. I personally feel that it is anything but lucky for the unfortunate horse made a slave to it. Here's why I've come to this belief. A horse in the wild runs and gallops on the open plains. Its hooves are constantly connected to the earth with each step. This connection causes those hooves to become harder over time which allows the animal to run further and faster over different types of terrain.

When this horse is captured by a human, the first thing the human does is forcibly hammer a metal shoe into the horse's hooves. This "shoe" is a slavery chain for the horse who cannot remove it. It elevates the horse's hooves off the ground where it is no longer grounded. The hooves become soft and tender without the rejuvenating power of the earth. After several years, when the horseshoe comes off, the poor horse is rendered unable to walk because of the intense pain of putting its hoof on the ground. A horse with one shoe missing will limp trying to keep that hoof off the ground.

This is not a lucky situation but a form of enslavement and forced dependency. Thus the horse has no incentive to run away because it will have to endure terrible pain and discomfort. However, in time, its hooves will heal and restore when it has been in contact with the earth long enough. If it would ever be made free by its owner. And a newborn horse should never have a shoe placed on its hooves, perpetuating the enslavement of its species.

How We Disconnect

I really don't understand how we as humans can be so easily misled by the world we live in. We wear shoes on our feet that are padded and insulated. Some of them are a few inches off the ground. These shoes we wear from childhood until we die.

Yet, these shoes prevent us from connecting with the earth because they are a layer between us and the earth. We are conditioned to believe that the earth is dirty and we should not walk barefoot on the earth. We are conditioned to think we'll become dirty by it. So in order to avoid getting dirty, we neglect the healing and rejuvenating power of the earth on our bodies.

Then we go back to our homes and spend our nights and evenings. The floor is made of wood or is carpeted. We are again walking on a barrier that separates us from the earth. If we have a backyard, it is most likely covered with grass or stone and we barely spend any time out there.

And so day after day, month after month, and year after year, we continue to live in a state of disconnect from the earth. Who made you think that you don't need the earth's energy?

Energy From the Earth

Here's a very pleasant example of tapping into the earth's energy. Consider when you go to the beach. Do you walk on the sand with your shoes and socks on? No, of course not. If you're like me, you take off your sandals and walk barefoot on the sand. You let the sand get on your feet and in between your toes. You also walk near to the water and allow the waves to splash on your feet near your ankles.

Don't you have a pleasant feeling after spending time like that on a beach? Do you ever remember a time in your life that spending time on the beach like that was not pleasant? If you are like me, you probably have no bad memory of just walking barefoot on the beach.

There is something almost magical about it. Do you ever notice it? Do you know what it is?

It's the connection to the earth that your body is craving. And this is not only anecdotal and feel-good stuff I'm talking about. There are actual scientific studies done since the 1960s to test the concept of our reliance upon the earth's energy. During the 1960s and 1970s, experiments conducted at the Max Planck Institute showed that human volunteers disconnected from the earth's energy developed all manner of physical abnormalities such as head-to-toe arrhythmia, hormonal issues, sleep disruption, and more.

The experiment showed that the earth plays a very important role in our internal biological clocks and functions. When totally disconnected, chaos ensues. When we reconnect, we allow the body to reconnect its clock to the earth.

To put it in modern-day perspective: Think of a computer on a network. There is one central computer on the network that is the timekeeper computer. It could be the server computer. When all other computers are turned on and connect to the network, they check in with that computer and synchronize their time to the main computer. So a computer can never be out of sync for very long as long as it can connect to the central computer. Now suppose you disconnect that single computer from the network and it was losing a second every hour. You may not notice anything for the first day or even week but in a month, it would be way off from the correct time. Suppose at the end of a month it was off by 10 minutes. Then someone comes along and reconnects it to the network where it communicates with the central computer.

Can you guess what will happen? Yes, it will sync the time immediately and be back on correct time again.

This is similar to what is taking place in our bodies. However, when we begin to connect to the earth again, the correction of issues is not immediate. Our body takes time to heal and repair itself. Yet, if we allow our bodies enough time, it will begin to show us remarkable benefits from earthing.

Everything Disconnects Us

The walls of our homes are made of wood and drywall compounds. These are not very conductive of the earth's energy and thus provide an insulating factor that separates us once again from the earth.

The beds we sleep on separate us too. The modern raised bed has its origins in ancient Egypt. The wealthy Pharaoh and his wealthy subjects could afford to have a platform raised on four legs to sleep on. The average working-class person would be sleeping at ground level on the ground. Carpets and special flooring also act as insulation from the earth's energy. There is just no escaping it in today's modern houses.

Some days I lament what our society has "evolved" to become. We are more sophisticated, yet we are in some ways more ignorant than our ancestors. In the abundance of book learning and schooling, many people have sacrificed their natural intelligence and intuition. So that even their mind is disconnected from the way of knowing the truth in the simplicity of life.

Matteo Tavera, a French agronomist, put forward the point of view that our human purpose was to live in alignment with the natural bioelectrical forces of nature. This force in nature governs the seasons and the behaviour of all animals and plants. Tavera gave examples of chickens, cows, and other animals comparing their wild natural states with their domesticated states. The chicken, forced to live in a man-made coop, is sickly and needs the use of antibiotics and other interventions. Yet the chicken that is living in a wild state will be healthier and more vibrant and rarely, if ever, be sick. A cow living in an insulated barn is made to feel colder on chilly nights while a cow living in the open field is more able to tolerate a chilly night. A cat or dog living in an insulated house like an apartment in a building will eventually become sickly and have its owner visiting the vet regularly for treatments while a feral cat or wild dog is rarely in such a sickly position.

Tavera, like me, lamented our modern lifestyle and how it disconnects us.

The Solution I Discovered

Earthing, using technology to mimic the real thing, in our modern-day home is something that is better than nothing. If you are stuck in an apartment building and can rarely get enough earth energy, then use the technology to help if it can.

While I was in California learning to build earth homes, I slept in one for a week. It was very humble by today's housing standards. In fact, it could be considered an emergency shelter. But it was the most wonderful experience that I've had.

Every day while there I usually went to bed around midnight California time. And I was normally up by about 4 am California time. Four am in California is about 7 am in Toronto. And I had an important call each day to make at 7 am to check in on things back home. After my morning phone meeting, I didn't go back to sleep but did some reading and meditation before getting showered and getting ready to start my day.

Each day was a long day of earth-home building. There was theory and practical aspects to the learning. It was hard work building for a paper-jockey like me. And some days my body was really sore from the lifting, mixing, and physical work. Side note: I got the best 1-hour massage for $20 from a massage place about 15 minutes' walk from the institute.

Back to sleeping in the earth dome. I found that my sleep in the dome was the most peaceful and restful that I have ever experienced. I awoke every morning recharged with my battery ready to go. The bed-womb (not bed room) was beautifully made and it felt like being in a womb. If you stretched out, you could touch an earthen wall at any moment of the night.

I'd find myself cuddling up to the side of the walls to sleep. The energy inside the earth dome was noticeable within me but I also noticed it with my smartphone. Inside the dome I'd be talking on it during my call. In the center of the dome the reception was not so good. Yet when I touched the smartphone to the wall of the dome, the reception was clear. When I mentioned it to a dear friend of mine, Ed Wilson, he suggested that the barb wire in the walls acted in a way that boosted the signal.

I also thought it was interesting that at the center of the dome, it was like being shielded, while touching the walls was reconnecting to the earth again.

I have to say that after that trip I fell in love with earth-home building because it showed me that it is possible for anyone to build them. Even someone with absolutely no experience can be taught the principles and concepts to build their own earth home. And you don't need a university or college degree to do it.

Why do people go to university and college? To get an education to get a good job. Why? To be able to make money to BUY A HOUSE and the things that go with a house. And a house is a large investment of hundreds of thousands of dollars.

What if you could spend less than $10,000 to educate yourself to build those earth homes and then spend less than $30,000 to build your own earth home? Would that short-circuit the mindless system? What if your earth home would last you about 100 to 200 years so that you never need to worry about moving and you'd have an inheritance for your children?

Does this sound like something that could open up a new world of possibilities and give you a new direction in life? And let's not forget the other benefits of being reconnected to the earth from which your body draws some of its healing energy and resets its biological clock and functions.

Bringing Your Heart Home

And quite honestly, this concept is so simple and easy to understand and to learn, that I stood on a beach one summer teaching it to my nine-year-old kid. We drew out a floor-plan right on the beach together. We planned where we'd like the bed-wombs and the kitchen and the entryway.

There's absolutely no reason why you should not get this going for yourself. If a nine-year-old can learn this, you've really got no excuse, have you?

Chapter Summary

In this chapter, I've told you about the disconnection we face and the way to reconnect again. I've shred with you some of the wonderful personal observations I have experienced in the earth homes, and told you that I was able to teach the concept to a 9 year old.

In fact, Nader Khalili designed the system to be easy and teachable so that disaster workers could go into any part of the world and begin build emergency shelters within hours using the earth on the ground.

Suppose an earthquake happened and people don't have homes? Drop off a team and they can get the people involved in building long term temporary shelters in hours. That's the beauty of simplicity and efficiency in the building system.

If a nine year old can do it. You can do it as well. If a paper jockey like me could learn it, then anyone can.

* * * * *

Vaughn Berkeley, MBA

Financial Impact of Earth Homes

Chapter 7

* * *

"It may be that the satisfaction I need depends on my going away, so that when I've gone and come back, I'll find it at home." - Rumi

"If homes were our most affordable investment instead of the most expensive, how different our societies would be." - Vaughn Berkeley

* * *

The money is the detail, isn't it? It's always about where you will find the money to pay for the things you need. In fact, it's one of the biggest influences in our lives besides God. Think of it. When you need food, do you pray to God or do you go get your money and go to the supermarket to buy food? You, like me, go to buy food.

Buying a house is the most significant financial decision a person will make in their lifetime. It has huge implications about the quality of their lives from that moment onwards. The ownership of a house is about moving money from you to various other people. Yet, when a house is acquired, even though money has been transferred, a new value is added by the ownership. A deserted house is valued less than one that is occupied.

In a previous chapter, I touched briefly on the financial implications of home ownership, but I want to compare and contrast the model and values for you here so that it hits you like a freight train. You will not be able to miss it.

Bringing Your Heart Home

The choice is as polar opposite as life is to death. But you, like me, and most of the 7 billion people on the planet have no concept of this. So buckle up and here we go.

To build an earth home, you start with the biggest raw material under your foot, that is, the soil. If you own the land, then the soil is yours free and clear. When constructing your earth home, you will be using the abundance of soil available on your property.

Major Material	Earth	Wood
Cost	FREE (Almost)	Expensive

With the earth, there is no cost to transport, prepare it, or anything else. It is truly free. With wood, which is used for framing the house and walls, you have to pay for the cost of a lumberjack to cut the trees, pay for the cost to cut and mill the trees into various types of wood, pay for the transportation of the wood to the supply store where you will buy it, and pay to have it brought to your site. What makes this worse is that all along the supply chain, you may have companies in debt to the bank. And each company is paying a debt service charge or usury on the loan. This cost is passed along to you, the consumer.

The next major material used is the siding on the house. This may be a brick exterior siding or another type of siding. This is another expensive item in the home. With an earth home, you are building the walls out of the earth. You may opt to make a plaster from the earth as well to plaster the walls, but this again is almost free for you.

Major Material	Walls (Plaster)	Brick/Siding
Cost	FREE (Almost)	Expensive

The roofing is another major element of the house structure. The earth home again can use the earth. In the conventional house, you have more wood, and the roofing tiles.

Major Material	Roof (Earth)	Wood/Tile
Cost	FREE (Almost)	Expensive

Next, the interior of the house has a cost. When building earth homes, can you guess what you'll be using inside of the house? Earth! You make an earth plaster and plaster your walls and floors. For a conventional house, you'd be using wood for the floors which would then be covered by carpet if it is cheap wood. Or you would have hardwood floors above the cheap lumber flooring. There may even be tiles in areas like the washrooms and kitchen.

Major Material	Interior Floors (Plaster)	Wood, Carpet
Cost	FREE (Almost)	Expensive

These are some of the tangible costs or expenses going into building a home. I hope you can begin to see it is greatly reduced with the earth-home structure.

When the house is there, wouldn't it be nice to have a swimming pool in your yard? Everyone has to pay thousands of dollars for a swimming pool. A person putting in a pool pays for the workers to dig and dispose of the earth, then build the pool. But a nice byproduct of building your earth home, depending on the size, is that you will have a hole in the ground which could be turned into a swimming pool for very little extra cost.

If the hole is not big enough, build a pool shed using more of the earth and voila, you will have extended the size of the hole for a bigger pool. If you need it bigger, then build a few more structures. And your costs are still very low with this form of earth-home building.

Now there are costs of building earth homes. It's not all free. You have the cost of the sandbags, the barb wire, and other materials or supplies you need for the house. But the amount of money you will be spending on this is minuscule when compared to conventional housing.

The tiny cost of building the earth-home structure and the swimming pool means that you as the home owner will not need to carry the huge dead-pledge (mortgage) that others carry. The ripple effect of this is that you will be paying less in interest on the mortgage, can pay it off faster than other people, and can begin saving your money for the other things that improve your quality of your life.

Insurance Protection Savings

Here's another huge financial implication of an earth home. Your earth home will be fire resistant, flood resistant, and tornado resistant, depending on the design. An earth house with an earth roof, could catch fire and burn. All the contents of the inside of the house could be destroyed by the fire. All you would need to do is clean out the ash, replaster the inside, replace the fixtures and fittings and you are good to go again.

This is huge. It means you can recover from a disaster like fire faster and more inexpensively than others with wood homes. And the financial bonus? You won't need to have a huge insurance policy on the home because it will not be expensive to repair. You will no longer be losing so much money to the insurance companies. In fact, if you saved that premium yourself in a tax-free savings account, you'd have money to fix up things on your own.

Legacy Planning

If you're a parent who wants to have a home you can pass on to your children that will not be a burden to them, then the earth home is a definite asset. And with a home life expectancy of 200 years or more, you'd be wise to leave one of these to your children.

Additions and Expansion

Suppose you started out as a single person with a piece of land to build your modest earth home. Then you found your soulmate and had a baby together. Suddenly, you find yourself with a need to upsize your dwelling place. What do you do? In a conventional house, you'd call the realtor, put up a "for sale" sign, and start looking for a bigger home. This takes a considerable amount of expense and time. The agent fees, legal fees, mortgage fees, and the cost of the new dwelling means you are deeper into the dead-pledge (mortgage) institution.

But if you are building an earth home with a modular design, you'd simply need to get more earth from your land, buy the materials for construction, and build yourself an extra room onto your existing earth home. Yes, it can be just that simple, convenient, and inexpensive. Plus you get the intangible benefit of staying in the home and community you love where you have built up valuable relationships.

Then in a few years, when you and your partner got busy and had two extra kids, you can create another add-on module to the home.

If you were an adult who wanted your adult kid to live with you or your senior parents to live with you, then you can easily add on an adjoining bachelor or parent pad. Or maybe you need a home office to begin working part-time from home. It is an easy thing to create an earthen addition for your home office.

The cost again is very inexpensive as compared to a conventional add-on to an existing home.

By now, I hope you are beginning to see the huge financial freedom that can be part of your future once you decide to go down the path of the earth-home building model.

In business, there is the principle of buying low and selling high. Financially, it makes sense to buy low into your inexpensive earth home. Then the value of it to your children or grand-children would be very high should they choose to sell. Think I'm kidding? Houses in the UK built from cob, an earth-based building technique, that are two- or three-hundred years old have sold for a million dollars or more.

The person who built the original cob house was probably not thinking it would be worth a million dollars in 200 years but there you have it.

A home is a good investment and an earth home is a freaking awesome investment in yourself and your future.

Chapter Summary

In this chapter, I've introduced you to numerous reasons why your earth home is the best investment of your life. I've shown where you could save money, plan your life, and leave a legacy for your children and grandchildren. There are so many benefits to building an earth home that by now, you should be getting as excited as I am about this.

* * * * *

Vaughn Berkeley, MBA

Environmental Impact of Earth Homes

Chapter 8

* * *

"Then a ploughman said, 'Speak to us of Work.' And he answered, saying: You work that you may keep pace with the earth and the soul of the earth. For to be idle is to become a stranger unto the seasons, and to step out of life's procession, that marches in majesty and proud submission towards the infinite. When you work you are a flute through whose heart the whispering of the hours turns to music. Which of you would be a reed, dumb and silent, when all else sings together in unison? Always you have been told that work is a curse and labour a misfortune. But I say to you that when you work you fulfil a part of earth's furthest dream, assigned to you when that dream was born, And in keeping yourself with labour you are in truth loving life, And to love life through labour is to be intimate with life's inmost secret." ~ The Prophet by Kahlil Gibran

"Humans leave an environmental footprint. Our duty is to make it as light as possible so the future generations can enjoy the beauty we have left them." - Vaughn Berkeley

* * *

When you work on building your own earth home it has some kind of mystical energy that cannot be fully understood with our present-day technology. It is as though you are fulfilling a part of your existence that you were meant to fulfill. On a spiritual level, you can feel it with each new layer that goes up in your home.

Yet, there is more than the spiritual. There are some tremendous physical benefits to building your own earth home and infusing it with your love, care, and attention. Here are a few of the other ways an earth-home building system can benefit you.

No Deforestation (for lumber)

Humans are destroying our trees for a variety of reasons. We destroy forests to create pastures for cattle farming to feed people meat. We destroy trees to make paper for newspapers, books, magazines, printing paper, cardboard and more. And we also destroy trees to make wood for housing construction. And it seems like there is no end to the need for people to live in houses if the suburban housing sprawl is any indication.

By switching even a tiny percentage (15 to 20%) of the houses built to an earth-based home building method, you could save a lot of trees that would have been used for the lumber. If you are concerned about the environment, then this is one way we can help the environment by not being a contributor to its destruction.

Hazardous Chemicals

A few years ago we ran a story in the magazine about toxic homes. Inside your conventional home, there are many different elements that are combined together to form a house. There are numerous plastics inside a house, numerous glues and adhesives, and different types of paints which also off-gas.

Even the cupboards and countertops that are used in your kitchen may contain formaldehyde as an ingredient in its production.

When choosing to build a home using earth-home building techniques, you may find there are many other ways that you can mould and shape the earth to create cupboards, countertops, and more. Thus, when they are well thought out and well planned, earth homes will greatly reduce or eliminate the toxins employed in the construction of the home.

Vaughn Berkeley, MBA

Relatively Long Shelf Life (Unlike Traditional)

When you think of the conventional home today, surely what comes to mind is the fact that you are expected to move to another house in 5 to 10 years. And when you move to a new house you will not see just how fragile your previous house was. This is deliberate societal programming to ensure that people never truly understand that conventional housing is designed, planned, and created with built-in obsolescence in mind.

Earth-home structures, unlike conventional home structures, are designed with the expectation that they will last 100 to 200 years. Which would you prefer? Would you prefer a house that must be demolished after 30 or 40 years because it is no longer in a state that can be repaired or would you rather be in a home that would last 150 years and that your children and grandchildren may be able to enjoy? The answer is obvious.

The earth itself has been around for as long as human beings can recall. It only makes sense to then build a home that is designed and created using the element known as earth. Even if the furniture and contents inside of the home become old and unusable, you can always replace them at minimal cost while your main structure is still as fully functional as the day it was created.

Earth as an Element

We touched briefly above on the concept of using earth as an element. There is a saying that I have heard and it says, "Earth turns to gold in the hands of the wise." This saying holds such hope for the average human being today because each of us can become wise in the proper usage of earth as an element.

Our dependence on trees as a resource for building is destroying our forests with the long-term risk of threatening our air supply and air quality. Trees after all clean the air and produce oxygen that animals and humans need to live. Everyone is concerned now about global warming, smog alerts and poor air quality in cities, and the ripple effect environmental changes have on ecosystems on the planet. And the earth is the most abundant natural resource that we as human beings possess. It is also fireproof, unlike wood. The reason why I believe we are not using earth as the fundamental building element of homes, is because there has been a social stigma attached to the earth.

While it is completely irrational, people may have imagery of Africans living in mud huts, or aboriginal people living in mud houses, and they tell themselves that they can never live in such an uncultured and barbaric way.

And yet when NASA was seeking proposals on the most cost-effective way to build on the moon, it was Nader Khalili's proposal to build on the moon using the soil of the moon that appeared to be the most cost-effective and the most expeditious.

We need to overcome the stigma that has been attached to the earth as an element and honour and appreciate it in such a way that we will begin to build again with this wonderful element given to mankind in abundance on this planet.

Bioelectrical Grounding

At one point in your life you might have heard the saying, "from the dust you are created and to the dust you shall return." Those words were spoken to the fullest created human beings on the planet according to the Holy Scripture. And in those words there is a hidden revelation about all connection to the earth. This connection has been discovered in the past few decades but is only starting to get some mainstream attention whereas it was on the fringes before.

The concept I speak of is that of Earthing. The fundamental principle of this concept is that the more you can connect yourself to the earth, the more you are able to draw from the bioelectrical healing potential of the earth. Because we are part of the earth and our bodies contain minerals that conduct electricity, when we ground ourselves to the earth, it helps the body to naturally realign its bioelectrical systems.

Science is not yet at the point where we can understand this concept completely. No one can understand how a migratory bird knows which way to go in autumn, or how tides impact the moods of some people, or even how the earth can impact our bioelectrical system. But we know these things happen.

I heard a story one time about an adventurer who went to the pyramids of Egypt and slept in the tomb of the pharaoh. He did it because he wanted to draw on some of the same energy that exists in that structure. I slept in an earth shelter for a week and it was one of the most amazing experiences I have had. I felt really charged each day after sleeping each night in that structure.

By living in a house made of wood, nails, plywood, carpet, and plastic, you are depriving your body of another tool that it needs in order to help it function at its best over time. This is one of the reasons why I believe every person should build a small emergency shelter of earth for themselves and dwell in it periodically.

The 4 Tonne Garbage Gorilla

Remember in an earlier chapter, we talked about how building a new conventional house generates a lot of waste. This is waste that the builder charges you by adding it into the cost of the project. Every foot of wood, every bent nail, every 1.5 feet of carpet or tile, every piece of broken drywall, you paid for it to be thrown out.

You're paying for creating and disposing of 4 tonnes of waste on your 2000 square foot home. How wasteful of you. But I can hear you telling me now, that you didn't have s single clue about that. And there are no other options available to the average person buying their first home.

And I agree with you on both fronts. No one told you that you were contributing to the landfill issues with garbage in such a huge way. And there aren't many options available to new home buyers with little knowledge and capital.

But times, they are changing. And knowledge abounds.

Wood typically represents 40% to 50% of all job site waste. Poor trees, poor landfills, poor future generations. But guess what?

Much of that waste is eliminated when you build an earth home because you mindset is totally different. You begin to think that this earth is precious and I can't waste any of it.

You use the earth for your outer walls and your inner walls. If you dig too much, is it wasted? No, you simple use it on another part of the earth home. Maybe there are no more walls to be done. Well what about the roof? Use it there. Maybe the structure is already up and now you have extra earth. Then sift it with a find mesh and create find sand to use for plastering the walls.

No waste in that regards. Now, I'm not saying the house will be zero waste. Depending on how elaborate you build it, you may have some waste with plumbing, or electrical but you can get on top of your plumber and electrician to monitor every details.

Now you've not only saved yourself 4 tonnes worth of money in disposal fees, but you've also been a good earth citizen and prevented add more garbage to a landfill.

Vaughn Berkeley, MBA

Chapter Summary

In this chapter, we discussed some of the environmental implications of the earth home. The 4 tonne Gorilla being one of them. You should take away that with earth building there are opportunities to recycle, reuse, and conserve the precious materials in your earth home.

* * * * *

Bringing Your Heart Home

Vaughn Berkeley, MBA
Build It and Your Life Will Come

Chapter 9

* * *

"Any woman who understands the problems of running a home will be nearer to understanding the problems of running a country." - Margaret Thatcher

"The peace and solace we seek is so close if only we understood the true meaning of home." - Vaughn Berkeley

* * *

Restoring Your Relationship to the Earth

Do you have a relationship to your current dwelling place? Everyone does whether they realise it or not. That's why horror movie makers make haunted house movies. They're attempting to cartoonify the relationship of human to dwelling place. If you don't understand the relationship you have with your home, they you may be missing out on key signs and symptoms of issues in your overall life. You've got to establish that relationship.

Safety and Security

One of the purposes of a home is to help the occupant feel safe and secure. The houses built today with wood offer very little to help the homeowner feel secure. Sometimes, a person can feel like one of the three little pigs in the fairytale.

The house made of wood is stronger than the house made of straw but it is still lacking when compared to the house made of fired earth or bricks.

A well-built earth home can even offer you some bulletproof protection if you live in an area that has a propensity for gun fights. I'm sure you've read some time about an innocent person being killed when the bullets ripped through the wall of their home and hit them. There would be no need to worry about bullets getting through a wall of earth 16 to 24 inches thick.

The design methodology could be adapted to refugee housing in war-torn regions. These types of earth homes would be safe enough to deflect any stray bullets that might come in that direction.

Tsunami, Tornados, and Earthquakes

A well-built earth home offers security against tornados and storms. It offers protection against earthquakes and tremors. The earth domes from California are built to withstand earthquakes. In fact, the government agency that have performed the certification and testing said the testing equipment had to be shut down as it was about to break as the earth dome stood firm.

Wow! That is extremely amazing.

These homes are not super-homes but they offer some protection. Imagine if a tsunami was approaching an island where you lived. You may live further inland and the wave would hit your home but not with the full force it had when it arrived on the shore. Wooden houses would probably be wiped out.

While the earth home built of a dome design would allow the force of the water to flow around the structure of the dome. This feature would disperse the force of the wave and may increase the likelihood of your earthen home surviving such a catastrophe.

This is one of the major reasons why I love this kind of building. The longevity aspect of it appeals to me.

Vaughn Berkeley, MBA

Global Warming and Prophecy

According to some ancient writings, there will come a time when the sun will be allowed to scorch the earth in various places. Conventional homes will be incapable of keeping the occupants comfortable in record-high temperatures.

Occupants will have their air-conditioning units running at maximum for long periods. And what will happen should that scenario play out? The government may begin to ration electricity in order to prevent large-scale power outages.

Then the heat will be unbearable for those who cannot afford to pay a premium for the use of their electrical air conditioner.

Only an earth home with a 12- to 16-inch thick wall made of earth can absorb the heat slowly over the day to heat the mass and release it slowly at night to maintain a consistent temperature. So the temperature inside the earth home during the day will be cooler than the outside temperature. And it will stay cooler longer without the need for turning on an air-conditioning unit.

Scientists are already sounding the alarm that the temperature of the earth is rising. And all the efforts of governments, industry, and ordinary people seem to be having little impact on the planet.

A problem that took decades to create cannot be repaired so quickly with the same kind of mindset that got us to that point in the first place. So given that the earth will be warming up and given that you or your children plan to live on earth another 50 to 100 years, how will you plan now for that highly likely future?

Will you buy a wood home and face all the same troubles as your neighbours? Will you be one of those forced to endure rations of electricity because everyone is turning on their air-conditioning at the same time? Or will you be the one prepared with a home that is aligned with the earth and heats up and cools down in alignment with the planetary forces and rules of nature?

It is the wise person who can plan ahead now for a relatively small financial investment. And given the rate at which home prices go up, I'd be hoping for a big payoff in 50 years or, if not for me, then for my children or grandchildren.

Chapter Summary

In this chapter, we touched on the importance of recognizing the relationship you have with your home.

* * * * *

Vaughn Berkeley, MBA

A Sample Project Plan for Building

Chapter 10

* * *

"The human brain now holds the key to our future. We have to recall the image of the planet from outer space: a single entity in which air, water, and continents are interconnected. That is our home." - David Suzuki

"The foxes have holes, the birds have nests, so you're pretty much assured of your home. - Vaughn Berkeley

* * *

Steps To Building Your Earth Home

Step 1: Get Your Land

The beauty of building using this new approach and seeking spirituality in the home is that you no longer need an excess of square footage. This is because you understand that more home does not equal more spirituality. And now you can focus on building the right home that suits your needs while keeping the land space available to grow a garden where you can feed yourself and your family.

Thus, for step one you need to find land. And for all purposes in redefining the home concept we only need one or two acres of land. Ideally if you were able to get two acres of land, then you can have your little piece of paradise on earth.

When selecting a piece of land, here are some things that I would consider. Does the land have access to a water supply on it? This could be a river that runs through it or it could be a well or it could be a government water source if the land is near to a road maintained by the government. The next question I would ask is whether the land contains soil for growing food. Another question I would consider is whether there are any chemical pollutants on the land. And for this you would need to do some soil testing at a laboratory. And finally I would ask whether I can afford it. You need a piece of land within your budget, but all things considered the overall budget for this type of home is a lot less than conventional homes built on a tiny lot and being sought for hundreds of thousands of dollars.

Once you are satisfied that the land meets your criteria, then you may go ahead and purchase it.

Step 2: Determine the External Factors Impacting Your House

Now you've got to look at some of the external factors that will influence your home. Maybe camp out on the land in a tent overnight and see where the sun rises. You can see if there are any trees that are blocking the sunlight. You can also get a feel for the temperature in the night and day. You can observe where the sun sets and whether there are trees blocking the sunrise and sunset. You can also determine which way the wind blows across the land. You can tell whether you have an east wind, west wind, southern wind, etc. If you have the ability to observe the water flow on the land during a rainy period, then you can also prepare for this aspect of the home. The more external factors you are able to document and observe, the better you are able to work with them instead of trying to fight against them and against nature. Trying to fight against it becomes a costly endeavour.

Making notes of all of these factors, you can position your house on the perfect spot on the land that maximizes your benefits while minimizing your effort and costs associated with the project.

Step 3: Determine Your House Size and Order Materials

Vaughn Berkeley, MBA

Once you've determined all external factors and you have your land, you need to decide what type of structure you plan to build. The beauty of using these good home-building techniques is that they are extendable. Think of it like building with Lego blocks. You can build a square with Lego blocks. Then you can add another square on to it later. With building earth homes, you can build your main structure and if your needs change over the years you can add on additional modules for your main structure easily with little cost.

For this book, I will presume that you are building a home for two adults. If I were building a home for two adults, I would consider a dome of about 16 feet in diameter. If we wanted to be fancy, we could build an app (a smaller 1/2 dome joined to a wall) that could be used for extra space.

Radius	Diameter	Square Foot
2	4	12.57
3	6	28.28
4	8	50.27
5	10	78.54
8	16	201.07
10	20	314.16
12.5	25	490.88

A single person on a tight budget may opt to build a 10-foot diameter home first then extend it later on. Once you have determined your size, then you can order the materials needed. The materials include the earth bags, the cement, and the barb wire. In order to determine the correct amounts you need, it is best to work with someone certified to build these types of structures or someone who has experience building one themselves.

You'll also need other things for the home which I'll list below.
* Plastic sheeting (like the kind used in greenhouses)
* Small rocks (also known as river rocks) for foundation
* Small gravel for your mixture if the soil needs improvement
* Wall outlets, pvc tubing, and electrical outlets if you plan on having electricity in your dome. I suggest you work with a knowledgeable electrician in order to spec out what you need and how to do it.
*A door and doorframe. If you build your own door, then you can save money, but if you want convenience, you can buy a door at the local hardware store and build your dome to accommodate the door.
* Fine sand and clay for plaster mix
* If you plan on a sink, shower or other water, then you need a plumber to help you determine your needed material.

Step 4: Design Your House on the Ground

Now comes the fun part. After you have ordered all your materials and you have an idea when they are expected to arrive, you can begin to draw your structure on the floor where you will be building it. You can take some chalk or even some white flour to map out your area. I suggest once you finish mapping out your area you start digging immediately afterwards. This is so that the rain or wind does not remove the markings you've placed on the ground.

Wherever you intend to build your dome, there you will find the centre spot of your circle and draw your circle on the ground. After you draw it, if you find you don't like the position of your dome, you can erase that line and draw again. You may do this a couple of times until you find the right spot that feels good to you.

If you are including some apps onto the main dome, then you can draw them in at the same time. Also you can draw in where you would anticipate your door and windows to be located.

Step 5: Dig Out the Foundation

Once you have drawn your structure in the earth, you can begin digging around the structure to create the foundation layer that you need to build upon. Another approach may be to elevate the entire structure if there is a risk of flooding on your property. That will require you to use more material to shape the land to a higher level that you can build on. But for the purpose of this simple plan we will assume the land is flat and you may proceed to build normally.

At this point you will dig out the foundation area for the main area and the apps that you have outlined on the ground.

Step 6: Build the Walls

The next step in this process is to proceed with building your walls. In order to build the wall, you will need to have your raw materials present. There is the earth mix you will be using, which will be a mixture of earth, clay, sand, gravel, and cement if necessary. There is also the barb wire that you will use in the wall.

The process of building a wall will be a slow and painstaking task depending on the number of people you have assisting you with your project and the height of the wall and the height of the dome. It will also depend on whether you are using long bags or pre-cut short bags.

Depending on the height of your wall and your dome, you may also need to erect some scaffolding once the height of the wall is above your chest height.

Safety must always be a concern on the project to ensure that all members of your team are wearing appropriate safety shoes and taking necessary precautions while building the wall.

Step 7: Build the Windows and Doors

As you are building your walls, you will need to position various frames in place so that the wall can be built around those frames. There may be tubes that will be inserted into the wall to create airflow. There may be a frame for a door that needs to go into the wall. There may also need to be frames for the windows that need to be placed into a wall. You also need to include space holders for your chimney, your water and sewerage, and your electrical.

The number of frames and placeholders you need to put inside of the dome wall will depend on the level of intricacy and the detail you have planned for your dome. You should work with a qualified electrician as well and a qualified plumber to ensure reasonable placement of the electrical and plumbing work in your earth home.

Keep in mind that the walls will be built over a period of a few days, and while it is being built the earth inside of the bags will be curing in the heat of the sun and the airflow. You can also install windows and doors once the walls have cured sufficiently.

Step 8: Build the Roof

Once your wall is up you have several options for building the roof. You may continue on building the roof using earthbags until you close off the roof. You may also opt to put in a roof that is supported on a wooden frame. This can be done in certain regions and with proper attention to structural details.

Having your roof of a material that is different from the wall may not be the ideal solution but it may be the one that is most appropriate given your particular circumstances. If you are going to deviate by using a roof made of wood or metal, then consult with a qualified building professional who will be able to assist you in placing the roof on appropriately.

Step 9: Plaster the Inside and Outside

Once the walls are up and the ceiling is on and the wall has had time to cure, now is the time to begin thinking about plastering the walls. The earth mixture that you will use to create the plaster for the walls will be of a finer texture owing to the fact that you want a smoother finish on the walls. You may find that you have to do this plastering two or three times in order to get a finish that is pleasing to you. If you have never done any plastering you may want to engage the services of someone who is proficient in doing plastering and have them assist you with the project.

Step 10: Waterproof the Outside

So now your dome is built and the plaster is on and you need to waterproof the structure in order to prevent moisture coming into the walls. There are several ways to waterproof your structure depending on where you are building and what kind of conditions you have to work with.

The thing to remember when waterproofing the structure is to try to do it all in a single run. Don't do part of it today and part of it tomorrow and part of it the day after. This is important because you want the entire structure to cure with its waterproofing layer at the same time.

Step 11: Beautify the Inside

Once you have completed the outside you can now turn your attention to doing the beautification of the inside of your earth home. This may involve installing the light fixtures and the sinks, painting the walls, designing all rooms and cupboards, and putting in finishing touches and trimmings to make your home look beautiful.

Step 12: Move In

And step 12 is to move in when everything is complete. This is the moment that you have dreamed about since you first started the project. It is the culmination of all your planning and all your hard work and effort. It is the realization of a dream. It is the manifestation of your will. It is your castle that you have built to enjoy in peace and security.

Congratulations to you on a job well done. You and everyone in your team that helped you deserve a huge round of applause and a pat on the back for being part of the movement to empower the individual on the pathway of housing.

Loved It: Let Me Know

* * *

I had so much joy putting this book together because I am passionate about helping people to lift themselves out of the present situation.

If you loved this book and you feel that we resonate together on the same frequency then get on my mailing list on CM Berkeley Media Group at cmberkeleymediagroup.com

I send out periodic email from time to time about other mind altering, thought shifting things I learn so be sure to link up with me on the site.

Also, if you liked this, you will love the book I co-authored on food. It's another mind bending experience that will make say hmmmm… The book is called "Fresh Food4Life" and you can find it on Amazon. It is part of the Holistic Health Nurse Series and there is a link to books in that series at the back of this book.

Bringing Your Heart Home

Vaughn Berkeley, MBA

About The Author

Vaughn Berkeley is the President and CEO of CM Berkeley Media Group, Co-Publisher of Canada's Premier Holistic Lifestyle Magazine for the Vegan and Raw-Vegan Community, the Gansta Gardener of his Block, and the Author of Two Books.

Under Vaughn's Presidency at CESAR, he established a perpetual bursary system for the continuing education students of Ryerson University which has generated over $1 million dollars for students since its creation. Vaughn was the recipient of the Hugh Innis Award for Human Rights and Social Justice.

Vaughn's also a professional photographer and you may have seen some of his photos published in EtenityWatch. Vaughn's a podcaster with a weekly podcast entitled, "The Berkeley Life-Biz Podcast" The podcast is a source of practical information for living every life, contains interviews with ordinary people who are changing lives around them, and lots of nuggets of wisdom.

Bringing Your Heart Home

If you know Vaughn by now, you'll see that he is a really humble guy who just wants to see people live better lives. This theme flows in whatever venture he is a part of.

* * * * *

The Podcast That's Reshaping Minds

By now, you've figured out that I'm not about following the rest of the crowd down the wrong path in life. I don't roll that way. This podcast was made to help anyone whose stuck in their life.

There's something for teenagers seeking to build on core fundamental principles, that can help anyone in their life. It also has principles that can help microbusiness owners, entrepreneurs, budding authors, and anyone whose been counted as being down and out.

The podcast is delivered weekly and you can listen to it on the website or via the iTunes podcast app. Every month, I feature an interview with an ordinary person who is doing something extraordinary in their lives. Just to prove to you that anything is possible if we believe.

Season 1 Episodes

001 The Berkeley Life-Biz Podcast Launch
002 Essential Time Management - Part 1 of 2
003 Essential Time Management - Part 2 of 2
004 Becoming an Opportunity Person
005 The 5 Habits of Successful and Wealthy People
006 Interview With Author Michael Lanfield
007 Making A Living Doing What You Love - Part 1 of 2
008 Making A Living Doing What You Love - Part 2 of 2
009 So You Want To Be An Author - Part 1 of 2
010 So You Want To Be An Author - Part 2 of 2
011 Interview With Author Betty Lenora
012 The Art of Setting and Achieving One Goal
013 Five Mistakes Successful People Do Only Once
014 Trapped Inside a Pyramid of Life
015 Interview With Author Richard Lalchan

Past performance = future performance? Only for people who refuse to grow and change. Your FUTURE is not related to failures of your past.

Strive To Be Your Best Today

~ Vaughn Berkeley

BERKELEY LIFE-BIZ Philosophy™

For great tips, insights, interviews, and more, check out our podcast
Listen on: iTunes or cmberkeleymediagroup.com

Vaughn Berkeley, MBA

Holistic Health Nurse Series™ Books

Volume 1: Eating4Eternity: Unlock Your Holistic Health Lifestyle™

If you feel that you are suffering prematurely from lifestyle diseases such as pain in the body, weight gain, constipation, tiredness, and what doctors call "getting old", then you need this book. It contains insights from Jenny, a nurse and health educator with over 23 years of experience in the medical profession. Her book will help you unlock that holistic health lifestyle that your body is aching for. Available in Print and Digital! Get it at http://amzn.to/wagvHC

Volume 2: Sweet Raw Desserts: Life Is Sweet Raw™

This book contains some amazing desserts for anyone interested in the vegetarian and vegan diets. The recipes are rawfood recipes, which are created without cooking. Some of the recipes require a dehydrator which removes moisture from the food. These are healthier recipe options to their traditional, cooked counterparts. Available in Print and Digital! Get it at http://amzn.to/MYer1e

Volume 3: Colon By Design: Overcoming the Stigma of Colon Sickness and Unlocking True Colon Health™ ISBN-13: 978-0-9868018-1-5

Jenny's passion for colon health has driven her to craft this excellent guide for anyone interested in keep their colon healthy. In the years to come, it is almost certain that this book will become the authority for ordinary people to turn to for health and wellness education. Available by the end of 2013.

Volume 4: Fresh Food4Life™: The Case For Taking Back Control of Your Food and Empowering Your Family and Community. ISBN-13: 978-0-9868018-2-2.

This next volume in the series takes a look at the most fundamental right of human beings on the planet. It is the right to have access to good quality food to eat and live.

Get it at http://amzn.to/Q8Zaf5

* * * * *

Forget the hype about writing your book in 3 hours, or 1 day, or even one week. You know that quality takes times, don't you? Learn our system to becoming a published author in 90 days? CM Berkeley Media Group has an online training program to help anyone aspiring to achieve this dream. Find out more about it and realize your dream at cmberkeleymediagroup.com/writeyourbookin90days/

* * * * *

Great Resources

EternityWatch Magazine (www.eternitywatchmagazine.com)

EternityWatch Magazine is the premier magazine for those seeking a truly holistic approach to health and wellness. The magazine is founded on the belief that good health is everyone's birthright and that by proper education, people can make the right choices to maintain their good health. The magazine is focused on plant-based nutrition, thus it caters to the rapidly growing vegan, and raw/living foods movement. You can get it free online just by signing up for it.

Eating4Eternity.org (www.eating4eternity.org)

Eating4Eternity is founded by Jenny Berkeley and is focused on her personal coaching approach. On the site, you will find news articles on health and wellness, Jenny's blog posts with her personal insights into what is happening in the medical field, paid courses and webinars, and some free information.

FreshFood4Life.com (www.freshfood4life.com)

Fresh food for life is part of living a healthy life. This website has information about a revolutionary garden solution for the home owner with no space. You can view videos, articles and order your own garden system. You can grow 24 crops in you very own kitchen. I have one of these and so can you.

E4Organics (www.e4organics.com)

The premier source for organic products online. Check out our wholesome organic items and place your order online today.

Hippocrates Health Institute (www.hippocratesinst.org)

Hippocrates Health Institute is the premier institute for alternative health and wellness. With over 50 years of experience in educating people to take control of their health destiny, the institute has a solid foundation. Their website talks about their programs, plus you can find copies of their magazine.

CM Berkeley Media Group (www.cmberkeleymediagroup.com)
This is the website for anyone interested in becoming an author. It contains some great insights into the writing industry, resources for new authors, and an online course to teach you how to write your book in 90 days. I use the techniques in the course to help enhance my system for writing my books. The course is worth 10 times what they charge for it.

Berkeley Centre for Nutrition and Development (International)
A non-profit dedicated to the uplifting of youth and adults via nutrition, development, and empowerment. http://bcndi.org

* * * * *

Vaughn Berkeley, MBA

Planning Pages

Use the following pages to help you plan your earth home project. Put your idea and rough plan here and then it's next to our reference book. Good luck my friend.

Bringing Your Heart Home

Vaughn Berkeley, MBA

www.ingramcontent.com/pod-product-compliance
Lightning Source LLC
Chambersburg PA
CBHW060845050426
42453CB00008B/845